ENERGY FROM THE SUN

Solar Power

James Bow

CRABTREE
Publishing Company
www.crabtreebooks.com

Crabtree Publishing Company

www.crabtreebooks.com

Author: James Bow

Editors: Sarah Eason, Jen Sanderson, and Shirley Duke

Proofreader: Katie Dicker and Wendy Scavuzzo

Editorial director: Kathy Middleton

Design: Paul Myerscough and Geoff Ward

Cover design: Paul Myerscough

Photo research: Sarah Eason and Jen Sanderson

Prepress technician: Margaret Amy Salter

Print coordinator: Margaret Amy Salter

Consultant: Richard Spilsbury, degree in Zoology, 30 years as an author and editor of educational science books

Written and produced for Crabtree Publishing by Calcium Creative

Photo Credits:

t=Top, bl=Bottom Left, br=Bottom Right

NASA: NASA/Jimmy Westlake: pp. 16–17; Shutterstock: Africa Studio: p. 12; Bezikus p. 15; Daleen Loest: p. 23; Elena Elisseeva: p. 11; Ferenc Cegledi: pp. 14–15; Filmfoto: pp. 18–19, 32; Fotohunter: pp. 10–11, 30–31; Imageman: p. 17; Jack Cronkhite: pp. 26–27; Leoks: p. 14; M. Cornelius: p. 8; Monkey Business Images: p. 28; Mrdoggs: pp. 6–7; Norgal: p. 10; Ozerov Alexander: pp. 3, 8–9; Pavel Vakhrushev: pp. 4–5, 28–29; Raulbaenacasado: p. 21; Shao Weiwei: p. 13; Sherwood: pp. 22–23; Ssuaphotos: p. 18; Tom Grundy: pp. 20–21; Wikimedia Commons: p. 7; Chixoy: pp. 24–25; Conserval Engineering Inc.: p. 22, GlassPoint Solar: pp. 12–13; Hideki Kimura/Kouhei Sagawa: pp. 1, 27; MrRenewables/Westmill Solar Co-operative/Neil Maw: p. 20; NASA: pp. 25, 26; NASA/EDO: pp. 3, 6: NASA/Joel Kowsky: p. 4; NASA/JPL-Caltech/Cornell: p. 24; Tatmouss: p. 19; Thecyrgroup: p. 9; E64: p. 16.

Cover: Wikimedia Commons: Hideki Kimura/Kouhei Sagawa.

Library and Archives Canada Cataloguing in Publication

Bow, James, 1972-, author
    Energy from the sun : solar power / James Bow.

(Next generation energy)
Includes index.
Issued in print and electronic formats.
ISBN 978-0-7787-1982-3 (bound).--
ISBN 978-0-7787-2005-8 (paperback).--
ISBN 978-1-4271-1640-6 (pdf).--
ISBN 978-1-4271-1632-1 (html)

    1. Solar energy--Juvenile literature. 2. Renewable energy sources--Juvenile literature. 3. Clean energy--Juvenile literature. I. Title.

TJ810.3.B69 2015   j333.792'3   C2015-903220-2
                                          C2015-903221-0

Library of Congress Cataloging-in-Publication Data

Bow, James, author.
 Energy from the sun : solar power / James Bow.
    pages cm. -- (Next generation energy)
 Includes index.
 ISBN 978-0-7787-1982-3 (reinforced library binding : alk. paper) --
ISBN 978-0-7787-2005-8 (pbk. : alk. paper) --
ISBN 978-1-4271-1640-6 (electronic pdf) --
ISBN 978-1-4271-1632-1 (electronic html)
1. Solar energy--Juvenile literature. 2. Power resources--Juvenile literature. 3. Clean energy industries--Juvenile literature. I. Title.

TJ810.3.B69 2016
 333.79'4--dc23

               2015020968

Crabtree Publishing Company

www.crabtreebooks.com   1-800-387-7650

Printed in Canada/032017/MQ20170208

Published in Canada
Crabtree Publishing
616 Welland Ave.
St. Catharines, Ontario
L2M 5V6

Published in the United States
Crabtree Publishing
PMB 59051
350 Fifth Avenue, 59th Floor
New York, New York 10118

Published in the United Kingdom
Crabtree Publishing
Maritime House
Basin Road North, Hove
BN41 1WR

Published in Australia
Crabtree Publishing
3 Charles Street
Coburg North
VIC, 3058

Contents

What Is Energy?

Everything in the world requires energy to move. You use energy to move your body, drive your car, and turn on your lights. Energy is the ability to do work. Types of energy include mechanical energy, in which simple machines such as levers and pulleys help you move things; chemical energy, in which substances react to each other; and nuclear energy, in which atoms are pushed together or broken apart.

Energy cannot be created or destroyed, it can only be changed, or transformed. If you burn a piece of wood, heat and light energy is created as well as **pollutants** such as smoke, ash, and **carbon dioxide**. Once changed, it can be difficult to change energy back to its original form. Energy sources that are easily used up, such as coal and oil, are **nonrenewable**. Energy sources that are not so easily used up are called **renewable**. Our ideal energy source is one that does not run out and does not create much pollution. Such a source is usually called "green energy."

The Sun hits Earth's surface with more energy every hour than people use in a year. Despite this, **fossil fuels** provide 67 percent of our electricity.

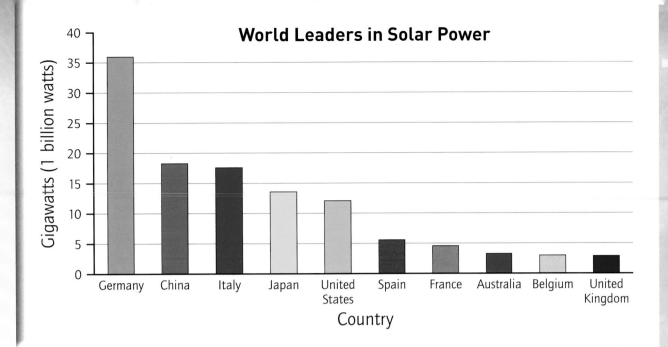

World Leaders in Solar Power

Gigawatts (1 billion watts) vs *Country*

Germany: 36, China: ~18.5, Italy: ~17.5, Japan: ~13.5, United States: ~12, Spain: ~6, France: ~5, Australia: ~3.5, Belgium: ~3, United Kingdom: ~3

At the Center of Things

The Sun is the source of almost all energy on Earth. The Sun provides heat and light energy. Wind energy is a form of solar power—winds blow because the Sun warms some parts of Earth's **atmosphere** more than others. Plants absorb the Sun's energy and store it in their cells through a process called **photosynthesis**. Fossil fuels such as oil, coal, and natural gas, or methane, are the remains of plants and animals that died millions of years ago, with the Sun's energy stored inside them.

In this book, we will look at how we can use the Sun's energy directly through solar power. By harvesting the energy of the Sun without burning plants or fossil fuels, we will release less pollution and the planet will benefit from this.

Germany is the world leader in solar power production. On June 9, 2014, the country generated more than 5 percent of its electricity from solar power for the first time.

The Energy Future: You Choose

Some people say that the Sun hits Earth with more than enough energy to power people's needs, so we would be foolish not to use solar power as our **primary**, or main, resource. Others say solar power is expensive to change into electricity, it does not work when the Sun does not shine, and we cannot depend on it. What do you think?

Solar Energy Is Nuclear Energy

The Sun is at the center of our solar system, 93 million miles (150 million km) from Earth. Despite this distance, the Sun hits Earth with 174 **petawatts** of energy each year. This is enough to power trillions of 100-**watt** light bulbs. The Sun is the biggest and heaviest object in the solar system. It is made up of 70 percent hydrogen, 28 percent helium, and 2 percent other **elements**. Inside the Sun, atoms of hydrogen join together to form helium atoms in a process called **fusion**.

An Ongoing Hydrogen Bomb

The fusion of every two hydrogen atoms into one helium atom releases enough energy to heat the Sun's core to 27 million°Fahrenheit (15 million°C), and its surface to 10,000°F (5,538°C). The nuclear energy generated by the Sun may be frightening to some, but fortunately we are far enough away that we are not cooked and not so far away that we freeze. The Sun's **radiation** arrives on Earth in the form of light, heat, and other energy, including **ultraviolet** light. Ultraviolet light is invisible to the naked eye.

The Sun has a diameter 109 times larger than Earth and has 330,000 times more mass. It accounts for 99.86 percent of the total mass of the solar system.

Around 30 percent of the Sun's energy is reflected off our planet into space. The rest of the Sun's energy, however, is absorbed and stored. It heats our soil and atmosphere to the point that Earth is not too cold to live on. Plants also absorb the Sun's energy through photosynthesis, using it to break carbon dioxide **molecules** into carbon and oxygen atoms. Plants use the carbon to grow and they release the oxygen into the atmosphere. Animals get the Sun's energy by eating plants that have absorbed the energy into their cells.

In 1797, Horace-Bénédict de Saussure tested a solar oven in the Swiss Alps. The oven worked just as well on the top of a mountain as at the bottom, proving that the air temperature around the oven played no part in the solar heating effect.

REWIND

In the 1700s, Swiss scientist Horace-Bénédict de Saussure created the world's first solar oven. He made an insulated box with three layers of glass, which collected the Sun's energy. On a sunny day, de Saussure was able to raise the temperature inside his box to 230°F (110°C). Can you think of other ways people have used de Saussure's design to trap heat from the Sun?

Collecting the Sun's Heat

On very hot days, some people say that you can fry an egg on the sidewalk. This is just a saying, however. Sidewalks do not heat up enough to actually cook an egg. However, there are ways technology can help make surfaces hotter. The Sun's light and heat can be reflected with mirrors. Glass lenses can concentrate that energy over a small surface, making it so hot that food can be cooked on it and water can be boiled on it.

Bending and Reflecting

Glass lenses that let light pass through, but bend it so that it is focused on a single point, date back to the 600s BCE. Some historians think lenses were used at that time to light campfires in Assyria, which is modern-day northeastern Iraq. The ancient Greeks knew how to bend and focus light. Around the 200s BCE, Greek mathematician Diocles showed that by curving a mirror into a **parabola**—a symmetrical open curve—the Sun's energy could be concentrated into a point small enough that anything placed there will catch fire.

A solar oven works by using mirrors to reflect heat. These ovens can reach temperatures of up to 752°F (400°C).

At the world's largest solar thermal farm in the Mojave Desert in California, 300,000 mirrors can generate enough electricity to power about 140,000 homes.

Since the **Industrial Revolution** in the 1700s and 1800s, fuel has been burned to boil water, creating steam that turns **turbines** to generate electricity. With mirrors and lenses, the Sun's energy can be used directly to boil water. Using the Sun's energy directly saves fuel and reduces pollution. Reflected energy from the Sun can be so intense that some modern power plants use it to heat molten salt rather than water. The salt can be heated far beyond the boiling point of water, so it can continue to boil water for some time after the Sun sets. This allows the power plant to use the Sun's energy even when the Sun does not shine.

REWIND

In 1666, Sir Isaac Newton took a glass prism and placed it in a beam of sunlight. He showed that sunlight is made up of all the colors of the rainbow. From this, we understand that the color of an object, like a red apple, absorbs most of the colors of light except for the color that it is—red, in this case—which it reflects. White objects reflect all colors. Black objects absorb all colors. If you want to absorb as much of the Sun's energy as possible, which color should you use? How can people use this in their daily lives?

Electric Light

We can harvest energy from the Sun more directly than heating objects with it. We do this through the **photovoltaic effect**. This is when sunlight, hitting certain substances, moves the **electrons** on the surface of those substances. This allows the electrons to break away from their atoms and become free, creating an electrical charge. Through this process, sunlight is converted directly into electricity.

Improving Technology

The photovoltaic effect was first observed in 1839 by the French physicist Edmond Becquerel. Becquerel placed two metal plates in a glass of salt water exposed to light and generated an electric current. Through the 1800s, scientists discovered other substances that had an even stronger photovoltaic effect. In 1883, the U.S. inventor Charles Fritts created a solar power **generator**. His generator was a solar cell using **selenium**, a nonmetal chemical element, and gold. It was neither very powerful nor efficient, but it showed the technology could work. In 1954, U.S. physicist Gerald Pearson helped create a solar cell using silicon. The cell generated far more power in a small space. By 1962, solar cells were being used to power the Telstar communications satellite. In 1968, inventor Roger Riehl created the world's first solar-powered wristwatch.

Solar panels can be used on many devices, from calculators to boilers used to heat water.

Big Power, Small Footprint

Since they were invented, the challenge of photovoltaic cells has been to generate more power in a smaller amount of space. The first solar cells were not very efficient at turning light into electricity. By the 1960s, however, solar cells were made with better materials such as silicon, and were much more efficient. In 1977, it cost $76.67 to produce one watt of solar power. By 2014, that cost had dropped to around $0.60, meaning large-scale solar power plants were much more affordable.

Many homes in the western part of the world now have solar panels made of solar cells to generate electricity.

The Energy Future: You Choose

There has been a debate over which solar energy technology is better—photovoltaics or concentrated solar power using lenses or mirrors. Those in favor of photovoltaics claim that by changing sunlight directly into electricity, solar cells are more efficient and flexible and can be installed anywhere, including rooftops. Those who prefer concentrated solar power note their technology is simpler and cheaper. Which do you think is better? Use examples from this book and further research to support your answers.

Other Things the Sun Can Do

Solar power is not only used to create electricity. The World Health Organization (WHO) has developed a way for people in developing countries to produce clean drinking water using sunlight. Plastic bottles filled with water can be left in sunlight for between six hours and two days. The ultraviolet rays in sunlight **disinfect** the water by killing any bacteria the water contains. More than 2 million people use this method to produce their daily supply of safe drinking water.

Water from the Air

The Sun can also be used to make salty or polluted water drinkable in a process called **desalination**. Anyone stranded on a desert island with a piece of plastic wrap could spread that wrap over a pool of standing water that is too salty to drink. The Sun's energy will pass through the wrap and cause the water to **evaporate**, leaving the salts and pollutants behind. When the water **condenses** on the plastic, it is pure, fresh water. In Las Salinas, Chile, a mining operation once used a large-scale version of this technique to produce around 800 cubic feet (23 cubic m) of fresh water each day out of mining water runoff.

Using plastic bottles and sunlight to make clean water is called the SODIS method. SODIS stands for Solar Disinfection.

Today, not only is solar power used to create electricity, but it is also used to help produce other energy sources. Solar thermal enhanced oil recovery is a way of using solar energy to turn water into steam to help extract oil. The steam is injected into an oil well to help push out more oil. However, by helping produce more oil, more pollution is created and more **greenhouse gases** are emitted. Can this really be better for the environment?

A desalination plant is like a power plant—both burn fuel to boil water—so both use a lot of energy.

FAST FORWARD

Saudi Arabia has a lot of oil but it does not have much fresh water. To get its drinking water, the country burns 1.5 million barrels of oil each day to draw seawater into desalination plants—there are 42 gallons (159 l) in one barrel. Saudi Arabia also gets a lot of sunlight, and in 2017 will open its first solar-powered desalination plant. The plant will be able to produce 2.1 million cubic ft (60,000 cubic m) of fresh water each day. Could Saudi Arabia's oil reserves have kept them from using solar power? Why might this be? How would Saudi Arabia benefit from using solar power?

Solar Energy by Design

We do not always need to build solar power plants or photovoltaic cells to benefit from the energy of the Sun. Changing the way buildings are built can help. Specially angled windows can let the Sun's light into a house or keep it out. Painting roofs black or white helps houses absorb or reflect more of the Sun's heat. This is called passive solar building design and people have been using it for centuries.

An Ancient Practice

The ancient Greek philosopher Socrates described building houses with openings that allowed the Sun's light and heat in during winter, and roofed porches that could shade those openings in summer. This worked because of the change in the angle of the Sun between the seasons. As Earth orbits the Sun, the tilt in its **axis** places the Sun lower in the sky during winter months and higher during summer. Throughout the Mediterranean and other hot places, buildings are constructed with light-colored stone or plaster to reflect the Sun's heat, keeping the interiors cool with no need for air conditioning.

The bright colors of these buildings in Santorini, Greece, are not only beautiful, but they also reflect the hot Mediterranean sun, keeping the interiors cool.

In the 1900s, computers and 3-D-modeling techniques allowed builders and architects to design their buildings to take full advantage of the changing position of the Sun in the sky. Since 1978, when the United States Department of Energy established solar-energy tax **incentives**, more than 300,000 buildings have been designed with passive solar energy features.

Regular roofs absorb the Sun's heat and radiate it, creating a "heat island." On a green roof, plants use the Sun's energy to help keep the building cool.

FAST FORWARD

Green roofs are another way to design a building to manage the Sun's energy. By covering roofs with plants, green roofs help keep buildings cool and absorb rainwater. On some green roofs, solar panels are The plants help make the solar panels more effective by reducing the dust and dirt that the wind blows onto the roof, covering the panels and blocking the sunlight. France has put forward a law requiring all new commercial businesses to be partially covered with solar panels or green plants. What benefits can you see from such a law? What would be the negative effect on builders?

Solar Power Problems

Some fans of solar power say that solar power is free, but they are wrong. Although the Sun's energy always falls on Earth, there is still the expense of collecting and moving that power. Solar cells cost money and energy to make. Silicon has to be refined from rocks, which are melted in a furnace. Other elements, such as phosphoros and boron, have to be added, along with a copper mesh to collect the electricity. Getting these elements costs energy and creates pollution.

Solar Challenges

It can be hard to generate solar power consistently. The Sun moves across the sky, so reflectors have to turn to keep facing it. The Sun is not out at night and clouds may get in the way of sunlight during daytime. Batteries can store solar power, but these are expensive to make and their production can create a lot of pollution.

The Aikawa solar power plant in Japan covers the equivalent of six American football fields. It is built on unused, inexpensive land.

Birds caught in concentrated sunbeams can burn to death. The light can also make them crash into the ground, where the injured birds might then be eaten by predators.

To generate enough solar electricity to power cities, photovoltaic cells must be laid out to catch sunlight, or mirrors constructed to reflect the Sun's light onto a boiler. Both methods require a lot of space. Solar plants can heat boilers to hundreds of degrees and the air around those boilers can become extremely hot. In 2013, as many as 233 birds were found dead at three solar power plants in California. Some birds' feathers caught fire in mid-air due to the reflected sunlight. The power plants themselves may also confuse birds, which mistake them for water. While the bird deaths attracted media attention, the number of birds killed by pollution from fossil fuel plants alone is estimated to be in the millions.

The Energy Future: You Choose

The problems solar power has experienced have led some people to suggest that the risks are not worth it and that they will only increase as more solar power plants are set up. Others say that all forms of energy have risks and costs. When comparing the problems of solar power to the health effects caused by pollution and climate change, solar still comes out on top. What do you think? Find examples in this book to support your answers.

Making Solar Power

We know that a lot of space is needed to generate enough solar electricity to power a city. However, unlike other sources of energy, solar power can be produced in smaller quantities—enough to power calculators, lights, individual air conditioners, and even buildings such as homes and schools. Photovoltaic receptors can be placed anywhere the Sun shines, including the roofs of buildings.

People are already installing solar cells on the roofs of their own homes. Some are turning to solar power to provide power in areas where power lines do not exist. Such places are called "off the grid." If power could be generated in the places where solar power is used, large power plants would not be needed. Long **transmission wires** that disrupt the local environment would also no longer be an issue.

The United States has more than 127.7 million houses, with as much as 6,184 square miles (16,016 sq km) of roof space. Imagine how much energy could be created if that area were covered in solar panels.

Solar Power on the Go

The idea that solar power can be installed anywhere has created smart uses of the technology. Solar panels are already used as a portable power source for temporary lights, road construction signs, and more. Parking lots in sunny areas have installed photovoltaic sunshades over their spaces. Not only do these shades generate electricity, but they also keep the hot sun off the cars underneath. They keep the cars cooler, allowing the drivers to use less air conditioning, and thus less gas. Using solar power in these ways allows cities to generate electricity without affecting people's daily lives. Few other green energy sources can do this.

A study by Berkeley University engineers suggests there may be 800 million parking spaces in the United States. Imagine how much power could be generated if the roofs of even half of these spaces were covered with solar panels.

FAST FORWARD

One company has produced a solar power cell that is **transparent**, or clear. This cell can be used in windows, allowing electricity to be generated as sunlight shines into buildings. Another company is looking at building solar panels that can be placed on roadways. These collect power and they could also change lane markers as needed, reacting to the traffic running over them. Are there places near your home where solar panels could be added? Why are these places suitable? What kinds of things do engineers have to consider when designing solar roadway panels where people will be driving?

The Solar Leaders

As the cost of producing solar power has gone down, its use is going up. In 2005, just 0.02 percent of the world's electricity—3.7 **terawatt hours**—was generated from solar energy. By 2013, that had risen to 124.8 terawatt hours, or 0.54 percent of the world's electrical power supply. There is still a long way to go toward replacing fossil fuels with solar power, but some countries are leading the way.

In 2013, Germany's solar power plants generated 36.013 **gigawatts (GW)** of electricity—enough to cover 5.3 percent of the country's electricity needs. China generated 23 GW, and Italy 17.6 GW. That same year, the United States generated only 12 GW.

The Westmill Solar Farm in the United Kingdom is owned by the local community. It produces enough energy each year to power 1,400 homes.

Solar Powers

For some countries such as the United States and Spain, solar power makes sense because parts of those countries are close to the equator and get a lot of sunlight and have few clouds. Other countries, such as Japan, turn to solar power because there are few other resources they can use. If oil and gas are not easy to get to and have to be imported from elsewhere, the benefits of producing energy at home makes solar power seem less costly than importing fuel.

For countries such as Germany, located far from the equator and getting little sunlight in winter, solar power still costs more to produce than other forms of energy. There, solar power was an investment made by the government through **subsidies** and tax incentives. The government and the people who voted for it believed the benefits of solar power, such as reduction of pollution and greenhouse gas emissions, were worth the extra costs of producing the power.

Deserts near the equator are good places for solar power plants. These regions have few clouds and get a lot of sunlight.

FAST FORWARD

In 2013, Germany added just 3.3 GW of solar power to its supply, compared to 8 GW in 2012, as the cost of new solar power projects proved too high. Other countries, such as Chile and South Africa, are increasing their solar production. Energy experts believe that the world should see 500 GW of solar power production by 2020. Given the advantages and disadvantages of solar power, which countries do you think will benefit the most? Which countries will benefit the least? How does the cost of technology affect the use of green power?

Midnight Sun vs Tropical Sun

Despite being far from the equator, Canada has increased its solar power production in the past few years. Starting with just a single **megawatt (MW)** in 1992, Canada was generating 1,210 MW of solar power by 2013. Canada might have short days during winter, but the longer summer days provide enough sunlight to generate a sizeable amount of solar power.

Less Power at the Equator

Countries closer to the equator have the advantage of high **solar insolation** (different from solar insulation). Solar insolation is the amount of solar energy that is received in a specific area. At the equator, the Sun is almost directly overhead. This means that countries near the equator are hit by more solar radiation than Canada is over the same amount of ground. However, very little solar power is produced in many countries close to the equator. For example, Brazil, with a population of more than 200 million people, produces 17 MW of solar energy—just 0.01 percent of the country's total energy needs.

A solar wall is used by the Greater Toronto Airport Authority to heat the air going into its Fire and Emergency Services Training Institute, reducing heating costs.

Solar panels provide power to these buildings in rural Africa without the need of costly power lines or a power plant.

Many factors contribute to the lack of solar energy produced by countries near the equator. Developing countries near the equator cannot afford to develop solar power. They may also not need a lot of power. A big solar power plant near the equator could generate a lot of electricity, but who would buy that power? More than 68 percent of the world's electricity is used by China, the United States, and the European Union. Most countries in the developing world do not have transmission wires that connect to the grids of countries that use a lot of energy, so these big consumers could not buy the energy.

The Energy Future: You Choose

Proposals to build large solar power plants near the equator mostly call for a host country—a country that produces solar power—to sell solar power to a country far away that needs the power. While the host country can make a lot of money, it will still have to handle the environmental disruption of building a large power plant and wires to carry the electricity. Is this providing the best benefit to the host country with the solar power? Does the host country need a big power plant to help its own people? Explain your ideas.

Solar Power in Space

Solar power is at its greatest beyond Earth's atmosphere —in space. Solar energy is the best energy source to power satellites and space stations. On March 17, 1958, the United States launched *Vanguard 1*, the fourth satellite to be put in Earth's orbit, and the first one to be powered by solar power. Although no longer in use, the satellite is still in orbit. The first solar-powered spacecraft was the *Soyuz*, launched by the Soviet Union on November 28, 1966.

All Clear in Space

Not only is solar power one of the only sources of energy available in space, but photovoltaic cells are also more effective there than they are on Earth. The lack of any atmosphere in space ensures that more of the Sun's energy gets to photovoltaic cells. This is because without an atmosphere, there are no clouds or dust in space to block the sunlight that reaches the cells.

Spirit is a **rover**, or exploring vehicle, which until recently explored the planet Mars. It was powered by solar power. Unfortunately, the dust of Mars eventually covered its solar panels and the rover shut down.

The International Space Station uses 250,000 solar cells on retractable 39 feet (12 m) wide "blankets." The cells can provide 6.6 **kilowatts** of power. Batteries store extra power, which is used when the station passes behind Earth and out of the Sun's light for 35 minutes of the station's 90-minute orbit. But generating all this electricity creates a problem—heat that can damage the space station's equipment. To deal with this, the space station's power system has radiators that are shaded from sunlight, and vent the heat into the cold of space.

The solar panels of the International Space Station (ISS) can provide enough solar energy to power 40 homes!

FAST FORWARD

Solar energy was used to power Spirit and Opportunity, the rovers sent onto the surface of Mars to explore it. Unlike the vacuum of space, Mars has an atmosphere that kicks up dust. With nobody around to clean the panels, people feared that over time dust would cover the solar panels and shut down the rovers. However, NASA was able to use the winds of Mars as "cleaning events," to blow dust off the rovers and keep them powered. Spirit shut down in 2011, but Opportunity is still going. If many parts of Earth become drier in the future, how might keeping its solar panels clean become harder?

The Challenges Ahead

Solar power can be used to heat water to turn turbines and electricity can be produced directly from sunlight. This is useful because it replaces the need to use fossil fuels to create electricity. However, it does not solve the problem of how to power cars, trucks, and other vehicles. Electric vehicles exist, but they cannot travel far from a source of electrical power.

The Helios is NASA's first of a kind, or **prototype**, for a solar power plane. It flew over Kauai, Hawaii, in July 2001, and was able to reach a height of 96,785 feet (29,500 m)—a record for a winged aircraft.

One idea to make solar power more available to cars is to use batteries, but these are made from toxic materials that are difficult to recycle. Batteries also take longer to recharge than it takes to refill a gas tank. Hydrogen gas could help. Produced when electricity is used to split water molecules into hydrogen and oxygen atoms, hydrogen gas can generate electricity using a **portable**, or movable, fuel cell. The challenge is to find a way to store hydrogen, which takes up more space than a similar amount of gasoline, in a tank small enough to fit in a car—without using **pressures** that could make the tank explode.

Power for All

Solar power is still a useful energy that can power buildings. Because each solar powered building has its own "power plant," there is no need for big power plants and long transmission wires that disrupt the environment.

Solar power is changing all the time and has come a long way in just a few decades. Scientists and businesses are researching new and better ways to get power from the Sun, so who knows how solar power technology may change in the next few years?

The Tokai Challenger solar car won the World Solar Challenge race in 2009 and 2011. It covered the course in just under 30 hours with an average speed of 62 miles per hour (100 kph).

FAST FORWARD

Since 1987, dozens of countries have competed in the World Solar Challenge. In this race, companies and universities build a vehicle powered entirely by solar power and race it over 1,864 miles (3,000 km) across Australia, from Darwin to Adelaide. In 2013, the race introduced the "Cruiser Class," featuring practical vehicles able to carry a driver and up to three passengers. Do you think such a vehicle could become commonplace in the future? Why would Australia be a good place to host such a race? Why is it important to hold competitions such as this? How might a vehicle such as this affect the environment and why?

Power Up!

Although the Sun generates most of the energy on Earth, most of the world's energy needs are still met by fossil fuels. If solar power could be used more, the result will be a cleaner world with energy we can rely on for centuries to come.

What Can You Do?

Until the technology to make solar power is improved and becomes less expensive, there are things we can all do to use less fossil fuel. This will help reduce pollution and greenhouse gas emissions. We can turn off lights when we are not using them. We can walk or take public transportation instead of driving. We can support companies that are already bringing solar power onto the grid.

Solar energy came about thanks to small steps taken by inventors, builders, and businesspeople over the centuries. The next steps are in all our hands.

We can all help reduce the use of fossil fuels by using public transportation more often.

Activity

Are you hungry? Are you ready to cook a hot dog with the power of the Sun?

You Will Need:

- A cardboard box around 6 inches (15 cm) wide
- A utility knife
- Posterboard
- A ruler
- A pencil
- Tape
- White glue
- Aluminum foil
- A skewer
- A hot dog
- Spare cardboard
- Adult supervision

Instructions

1. Trace a curve on the two long sides of your cardboard box, starting at the open end. The curves should run from the edges at each end of the box and should be about 2 inches (5 cm) deep in the middle.
2. Carefully cut out the curves with the utility knife. Ask an adult for help.
3. Measure and cut the posterboard so it fits over the open end of the box and the curves you have cut. Tape the posterboard into place.
4. Cover the posterboard with white glue. Apply aluminum foil with the shiny side facing outward. Take care not to leave any wrinkles. Start in the middle and smooth toward the edges.
5. Find the spot in front of your box where the light is focused, either by testing it against your hand, or another piece of cardboard. Then tape a spare piece of cardboard on each side of your box, near the middle, extending out to the focal point. They should stand upright. These are your supports. Mark this spot on your supports, and make a hole through the marks.
6. Carefully place your hot dog on a skewer and push each end of the skewer through the holes in the supports.
7. Turn the hot dog until it is thoroughly cooked, then enjoy! Do not leave the hot dog unattended outside.

Glossary

Please note: Some bold-faced words are defined where they appear in the text

atmosphere The layer of gases that surround Earth

atoms The smallest possible parts of an element

axis The imaginary line around which an object such as Earth rotates

carbon dioxide A gas molecule made up of a carbon atom joined with two oxygen atoms

condenses When a gas changes to a liquid

desalination Removing salt from water

disinfect To kill harmful bacteria

electrons Tiny particles with a negative charge that move outside the nucleus of an atom

elements Basic substances that cannot be broken down further; Elements make up all the matter in the world.

evaporate When a liquid changes to a gas

fossil fuels Energy sources made from the remains of plants and animals that died millions of years ago and were buried

fusion When two or more things chemically or mechanically combine into one

generator A machine that changes motion into electrical energy

gigawatts (GW) Units of measure for energy; There are 1 billion watts in a gigawatt.

greenhouse gases Gases in the atmosphere that contribute to the greenhouse effect

incentives Things that encourage people to do certain things

Industrial Revolution A rapid change in which countries become more focused on using machines to make goods

kilowatts Units of measure for energy; There are 1,000 watts in a kilowatt.

megawatt (MW) Unit of measure for energy; There are 1 million watts in a megawatt.

molecules Two or more atoms joined together

petawatts Units of measure for energy; There are 1 quadrillion watts, or 1,000 gigawatts, in a petawatt.

photosynthesis A process in which plants use sunlight to make food from carbon dioxide and water, creating carbon atoms that they use to grow and releasing oxygen into the atmosphere

photovoltaic effect An effect in which certain substances generate electricity when exposed to light

pollutants Substances released into the environment that are harmful or poisonous to plants, animals, or people

pressures The forces produced when something presses or pushes against something else

radiation Waves of energy sent out by sources of heat or light, such as the sun, or by radioactive materials

receptors Things that take in or absorb something

subsidies Payments made to reduce the cost of an activity

terawatt hours Getting 1 terawatt (one trillion watts) of power for one hour

transmission wires Wires that move electricity from the power plant to the people who use it

turbines Machines in which a rotor is made to turn by the power of the wind, moving water, or by steam

watt Unit of measure for energy; Watts measure the power used by an electrical appliance or device.

Learning More

Find out more about alternative energy and solar power.

Books

Doeden, Matt. *Finding Out About Solar Energy.* Minneapolis, MN: Lerner Group, 2015.

Hantula, Richard. *Solar Power.* New York, NY: Chelsea Clubhouse, 2010.

Oxlade, Chris. *Solar Power.* Chicago, IL: Raintree, 2012.

Websites

Conduct solar-related experiments with SolarTownKids at:
http://solartownkids.com

Explore facts about the Sun, solar power, and the environment at:
www.eia.gov/kids/energy.cfm?page=solar_home-basics

Learn about the environment, play games, and do eco-related activities at:
www.ecokids.ca

Index